# Gold Digger Words

of

# Hz. Mevlânâ Jelâleddin Rûm-î

translated from

Hz. Mevlana`Dan Güzel Sözler
a commemorative of the author's 800th birthday

Petama Project Editions, Zürich

Füchslin Puran

# Gold Digger Words
# of Hz. Mevlânâ Jelâleddin Rûm-î

translated from:
Hz. Mevlana'Dan Güzel Sözler
a commemorative of the author's 800th birthday

Zürich: Petama Project Editions, Zürich, 2016

| | |
|---|---|
| Published by: | Petama Project, Puran Füchslin<br>Kanzleistrasse 151, 8004 Zürich<br>Email: puran@petama.ch<br>www.petama.ch |
| Design and Layout: | Petama Project, Zürich |
| Production: | Books on Demand, Norderstedt<br>www.bod.de |

1st edition by Petama Project
Copyright © 2016 Puran Füchslin

ISBN 978-3-907643-25-9

Bibliografische Information der Deutschen Nationalbibliothek:
Die Deutsche Nationalbibliothek verzeichnet diese Publikation
in der Deutschen Nationalbibliografie; detaillierte bibliografische Daten
sind im Internet über http://dnb.d-nb.de abrufbar.

# Foreword

'Gold Digger Words' are aphorisms of Hz. Mevlânâ Jelâleddin Rûm-î. At the occasion of the 800th birthday of the great Sufi, a commemorative was published in Turkey under the name 'Hz. Mevlana Dan Güzel Sözler' - this is how the original looks like:

Eight years later a dear friend gave me a copy as a present, and I carried it with me, tried to understand the English translation in the original. 'Güzel Sözler' means 'Beautiful Words'; and in the course of the first nine months of this year 2016 I began to wash out the meaning of these words, as the gold diggers did in the pioneer times of the USA.

Today we have a Swiss website which offers panning for gold courses as a pastime (http://goldwaschen.ch) - there we can learn the techniques, there is a panning calendar, a club panning, and a European Championship, Rules and Golden Links.

That was the method. If you, dear readers, are more familiar with the Turkish language as I am, please forgive me, if you still find sand grains among the Golden Words - they must be ascribed to my shortcomings, not to the words of Hz. Mevlânâ.

I would like to describe of what this panning work consisted, with an example. We know such short, concise sentences well here in Switzerland, such as:

> **'De Joggeli sött go Birli schüttle,
> und d'Birli wänd nöd falle.'**

How could we explain to the many refugees who have stranded here between the worlds, our joy about the wit and the precision of this sentence? ('Jack should shake down pears, but the pears have no desire to fall'). It contains almost half a Swiss life, a thousand things which we do not need to describe, because we have this one sentence.

In the heart of each country such sentences are anchored, and no language study would help us to reproduce the fullness of the content which such a 'Beautiful Word' can mean to someone who has grown up in the heart of this country.

So I would like to describe you here, what was at my disposal as raw material, what was collected in pans and sieves. Point of departure is the original in Turkish (Hz. Mevlânâ Rûm-î himself spoke Farsi and Arabic, he was familiar with medicine, architecture, astronomy, mathematics - as all scholars of his time. His writings are composed in these language, in Konya he was called 'the foreigner')

> **Ayıpsız dost arayan, dostsuz kalır.**

The English translation in the books words:

> **One who prefers friend without having shame,
> he can become alone without having friend.**

To come closer to the understanding of the Turkish language, I toggled the same sentence into Google Translator:

> **Seeking friendly non-defective, it remains friendless.**

Next attempt: I toggled each words into Google Translator, here the results:

Ayıpsız - non-defective
dost - friend
arayan - caller, seeker, searcher
arayış - seeking
dostsuz - drab, unfriended, unbefriended
yurtsuz - homeless
susuz - anhydrous, waterless
susuz - thirsty, dehydrated
kalır - remains
kalıp - mold, cast, pattern, template, cake
kalın - thick, dense, stout, grave
dark, limited, slow-witted

I learned so much during these nine months; wonderful, how richly faceted the Turkish language is, what an immense thesaurus it embraces, how subtly we should really listen, before we could say: 'I understand the people whose mother tongue is Turkish'. And how thousands of imperfections in my understanding maybe have nevertheless lead me to the vicinity of the paths, of whose I think that they have unveiled to me the meaning of a 'Beautiful Word'.

If you, dear friends, perceive that it still 'scrunches of sand while reading', please wash a little more in the sieve - thank you for your love and forbearance. I left away a few aphorisms - despite of all panning and sieving they kept scrunching, and so I capitulated.

But very often the beauty and clarity of Hz. Mevlânâ flared up, and the simplicity of his images began to shine. Just like a diamond we can look at them from different angles, each time new aspects come into light. It is our work to uncover beauty within. With each aphorism I have left its title in Turkish.

\* \* \*

There are a row of things of which I feel ashamed; about us, what attitude we hold before we look and try to understand; how easily we expose 'other behaviours' to our fast judgment, how little we are able to perceive - beyond this frame - subtlety, life, human qualities.

I am so deeply grateful for the present of 'Dost' - thank you so much, dear Necati. You can bring me close compassion and understanding, in a language and culture in which I have not grown up; thanks to you I can trace the feelings, how such a sentence can be a help for survival. When I as an adult stumble through ruins of what was my home town and I know, that it will take me three hours to get a bucket of water; and when I worry about my child who lies at home with fever - I can assess when his situation will worsen, effect of dehydration. Then a sentence like this makes sense:

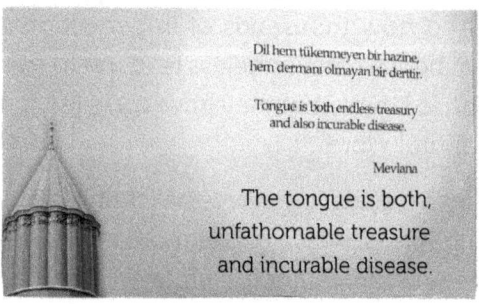

Does such a 'Beautiful Word' alleviate fever and the thirst of a child? I trust that it can contribute, not the word alone; we must stand behind it as human beings, and wish to act. It is for this reason and for this purpose I have translated here.

A most heartfelt 'thank you', dear friends, for your sympathy, your forbearance and your understanding.

Zürich, beginning of October 2016        Puran

# Güzel Sözler

### Dünya - World

The worldly life is not loyal;
it will leave you;
don't attach your desires to it.
Try to leave the world before it leaves you.

### Mahşer - Last Judgment

Sleep and the moment of awakening
are a form of a small last judgment.

### Olgunluk - Maturity

It is maturity which inquires firstly into your ego
what it wishes to do – and then does the opposite,
of what the ego desires.

### Anlamak - Understanding

If someone speaks sweet words,
listen to the tone within
and understand.

### Söz - Word

A word can be uttered only once.
It is like an arrow which is launched from the bow;
the arrow will never come back.

## Söz - Word

A truthful word brings relief to the soul.
Truthful words are morsels of decoy for the wish.

## Olgunluk - Maturity

My whole life is not more than these three words:
I was raw, I was cooked, and I was burnt.

## Haddini Bilmek - Know your Limits

The crow shouts loudly in the garden.
So the nightingale suspends her song
because of the crowing.

## Aç Insan - The hungry Human Being

Two kinds of human beings are always hungry:
the one who pursuits science,
and the other who runs after money.

## Özür - Apology

The apology of a hypocrite
cannot be accepted,
because it only comes from words,
not from the heart.

## Konuşmak - Speaking

Depth in the word arises from few words;
talking is like bark,
when there is much talking, it loses its core.

### Olgunluk - Maturity

Sainthood cannot be reached because of grey hair
and a grey beard. Who is older than the devil?

### Dert - Trouble

In this world there are many fools,
they give a skirt full of gold to the devil
and in doing so they buy their own discomfort.

### Asalet - Nobility

Can a stone turn green because spring is here?
Turn into fertile soil, and you will bring forth
flowers of various colours.

### Susmak - Holding Silence

To hold silence is like the ocean,
speaking is like a river.
When the ocean is looking out for you,
you will not seek for the river.

### Yönetici - Potentate

When fools are in power,
the wise keep themselves under the rug,
if they fear them.

### Insan - Human Being

I saw human beings who had no clothes;
and I saw many clothes,
and there were no human beings inside.

### Aşk - Love

As long as our hearts do not burn with tears of love,
there will be neither water nor fire on earth.

### Aşk - Love

A true lover shines out
among a hundred people
like a luminous moon among the stars.

### Aşk - Love

Love is like the endless ocean;
neither is there a beginning nor an end.

### Kapasite - Capacity

We have no right
to proclaim an ocean as guilty,
when we only have a small mug.

### Idrak - Understanding

Whatever you might know,
your words will remain limited
within the frame of understanding
of the one who listens to you.

### Azim - Presence

An fragile shell cannot hold its pearl.

## Uzmanlık - Expertise

Let us assume that you have inherited Zülfikar,
the sword, from Ali. But if you do not have
Ali's heart and arm, what will be it's use?

## Kötülükten Kurtulma - Deliverance from Evil

Oh my soul,
first mend the damages of the mouse,
then begin to gather the wheat.

## Arzu - Desire

Whether you go slow or fast,
when you are looking for something,
at the end you will reach the desired goal.

## Asalet - Dignity

Did you ever harvest barley
when you had sowed wheat?

## Takım çalışması - Teamwork

How can the green grass be happy,
when the clouds do not cry?

## Yönetici - Potentate

A ruler is like a pool,
all others are like water pipes
leading to the pool.

### Idrak - Knowledge

The Day of Judgment
is a terrible holiday of sacrifice;
for the believers it is a day of festivity,
for the oxen it is death.

### Dünya - World

The world is a trap, fed by desire.
Avoid the trap of desire.

### Başarı - Success

Three things are necessary for a successful life;
Attention, regularity, perseverance.

### Dünya - World

The world is not a suitable toy for the wise,
but a valuable swing for the foolish.

### Hata - Fault

Down at the bottom of the ocean
we find pearls and pebbles together,
valuable things among faults and errors.

### Ticaret - Trade

When you are not a master in trading,
don't open a store;
to become a master, you must be kneaded,
and be under the command of someone else.

### Uzmanlık - Expertise

When you have skills in art,
and you do not look for a master to orientate,
you will be looked at as a clown in towns and villages.

### Idrak - Cognition

For a donkey there is no difference
between a pearl and a pebble;
more than that, a donkey doubts
if there can be a pearl and an ocean.

### Öz - Essence

Do not worry
when the shell breaks,
the pearl is inside.

### Takım çalışması - Teamwork

When black wood connects with fire,
the black colour in the wood
disappears and turns into light.

### Başarı Merdiveni - Ladder to Success

When in chess
a pawn moves straightforward,
in the end he will become a queen.

### Azamet - Greatness

When a bird settles on a mountain
and then flies away and goes too far,
eager to look and see,
there is neither lack nor excess with the mountain.

### Asalet - Nobility

There is no difference;
if a shabby dog
wears a gold collar or a woollen collar,
he remains a shabby dog.

### Bilgi - Knowledge

When it comes to knowledge,
the feet become like wings.

### Bilgi - Knowledge

Knowledge is a limitless ocean,
the one who looks for knowledge
is like a diver into that ocean.

### Akıl - Mind

The suffering of a caring being
is better than loyalty of an ignorant.

### Eylem - Action

Attaining knowledge comes through words,
learning art comes through doing.

### Akıl - Mind

In the beginning of understanding
the brain storms easily,
but the ignorant bounce
their heads against the wall.

### Sormak - Enquiry

Both, question and answer,
arise from knowledge.

### Iyi Huy - Good Behaviour

I roamed the whole world,
but I could not find any higher merit
than good behaviour.

### Kötüler - Villains

When good people leave,
beautiful memory remains,
but the bad leave
cruelty and damnation behind.

### Asalet - Nobility

Two kinds of bees feed
from the same flowers;
one produces honey,
the other produces poison.

### Dindar - Devotion

Believer, stay away from the hostile,
look for the one who lives with God,
sit close to him.

### Gönül - Heart

You will find vineyards, gardens
and green fields in your soul,
her outside is like a reflection on the water.

### Kötü Huylar - Bad Character

Arrogance, passion and greed,
all smell alike,
the smell of onion when you speak.

### Özü Sözü Bir - Righteousness

Even when someone has
hundreds of expressions at his disposal;
if his heart and speech are not one,
he will say nothing.

### Zenginler - the Rich

The smell of a cesspool is a hundred times more bearable
than to converse with rich people whose soul is rotten.

### Ahmak - Fool

You are looking for the smell of roses,
and you stick your nose into garlic.

### Iyiler–Kötüler - Good People and Villains

The villains commit their impurities;
but in any case,
water does its best to clean them.

### Dalkavukluk - Flattery

When you glorify evil
you will cause the throne to tremble.

### Kötü Huylar - Bad Character

A good and beautiful appearance
in company of bad habits
is worth less than a false cent.

### Zulüm - Cruelty

Do not beat the iron of cruelty
against the stone of cruelty,
because like man and woman
they will give birth
to a new generation of cruelty.

### Dost - Friend

The one who leaves someone for you,
will also leave you for someone else.

### Düşünce - Thought

If you welcome evil thoughts
they will work as a poisoned nail;
they grow and will leave deep scars in the face of life.

### Benlik - Egoism

Feel compassion with the evil and bad people;
but don't blow up your ego
and don't make it your show.

### Kötüler - Villains

Don't be afraid of evil, do not take part in it;
it is like a germ, and God surely will eliminate it.

### Asalet - Nobility

If you teach science and wisdom
to someone with an evil heart,
it is like giving a sword to a mob;
it will bring about terror.

### Dost - Friend

If friends and relatives cause cruelty,
it is like three hundred thousand cruelties of enemies.

### Dost - Friend

The one who seeks perfect friendship,
can also stay alone without any friend.

### Öz - Essence

Not in every shell
you will find a pearl.

### Arkadaş - Companion

If you wish to get acquainted with someone,
look who are his closest friends.

### Dost - Friend

If you do not have a friend,
why don't you look for one?
When you have found a friend,
why are you not happy with him?

### Dost - Friend

Whoever has a true friend
does not need to look into a mirror.

### Arkadaş - Companion

When a poisonous snake bites
a human being, he will die;
but an evil companion takes him
to hell and to eternal damnation.

### Dost - Friend

When you become a friend,
you will have countless friends.
If you don't become a friend,
you will stay alone,
with no friend and no help.

### Dost - Friend

Become a friend of human beings;
then the caravan will reach more people
and the influence of the masses will reduce.

### Arkadaş - Companion

When you are far away from your companion,
you cannot express yourself,
not even with a hundred speeches.

### Ahmak - Fool

Friendship with a fool is worse
than having an enemy;
stay away from a friendship with a fool.

### Israf - Squander

When you take water from the ocean,
you should care to give it new water;
if not you will turn the ocean into a desert.

### Cömertlik - Generosity

Before the angel of Death takes all from you,
it is wise to return all things
which you have been granted before.

### Nefis - Ego

Our ego is like a thorn with three sides to it;
in whichever direction you turn it,
it will still prick you.

### Nefis - Ego

Your enemy also uses friendly words
which flatter you, they serve as a bait.

### Eğitim - Education

When a candle lights another candle,
its light will not lose any of its strength.

### Cehalet - Ignorance

If you don't know the blacksmith
when you are passing by his fireplace,
your hair and your beard might get burnt.

### Doğruluk - Justice

The straight path awakens the fullness of feelings;
and desire tames itself into feelings.

### Doğruluk - Justice

No matter how much water flows through a creek,
the reflection of the stars always remains the same.

### Doğruluk - Justice

The straight path is as the rod of Moses,
the twisted path is like the wand of a magician.
When the straight path appears,
it absorbs all crookedness.

### Akıl - Mind

When you wish to use your brain,
look for a friendship with another man of brain,
so you can learn by consulting each other.

### Dost - Friend

If you help a person with evil intentions,
be watchful, your friendship might be in vain.

### Dinlemek - Listen

It is wise to listen first,
before you wish to say something;
then you can refer to what you have heard.

### Sevgi - Love

When you give,
be generous and helpful like a river.
In compassion and grace
be like the sun.
When you hide the fault of your friend,
be like the night.
When you are angry and furious,
be like dead.
In modesty and humility
be like the earth.

So be either your essence
or be your outer appearance.

### Doğru söz - Right Word

You can always say the right thing,
but don't say the right thing all the time.

### Akıl - Mind

A human being can become a personality,
but not by dyeing his hair and his beard grey.

### Öfke-Kin - Anger, Hatred

Anger and passion
cause people to squint;
the spirit detaches itself from truth.
When hatred appears, you lose your skills,
and a veil covers the soul from your eyes.

### Dert - Trouble

Trouble is an ambling horse;
it will carry you to more trouble.

### Görüş Açısı - Viewpoint

We can be thankful to God
that He created roses among the thorns,
instead of complaining
about thorns among the roses.

### Tembellik - Laziness

When there is benefit, it comes from our effort and work,
but when there is loss, it comes from our idleness.

### Burnunun dibini Görememek -
### Blind for what is right under our nose

Pharao gave order to kill a hundred thousand,
but the one who he was looking for
lived in the garden of his palace.
Water in the ship makes it drown,
water under the ship carries it.

### Usul–Üslüp - Procedure - Style

Where there is need, there goes the remedy;
where there is a receptacle, water is collected.

### Gönül - Heart

Wisdom of the heart carries its owner,
but outer knowledge becomes a burden to him.

### Sevgi - Love

Illness is cured with compassion,
A dead body is revivified by compassion,
a Sultan turns into a servant through compassion.

### Sevgi - Love

Love and compassion
are signs of human life,
anger and lust
are signs of animal life.

### Zulüm - Cruelty

Cruelty of a demon
is like a dark well;
but the well of cruelty itself
is even more horrible.

### Zulüm - Cruelty

Hey you, who are digging a well of cruelty!
You are preparing a trap for yourself!

### Öğüt - Advice

The grinding work on ourselves does not automatically
bring about the scent of musk
when we are accustomed to bad smells.

### Şükür - Gratitude

Gratification makes human beings fall asleep,
but thankfulness wakes us up.

### Gönül - Heart

The range of vision of our mind reaches until our grave;
the vision of the soul can reach until the Day of Wonder.

### Akıl - Mind

When the Sultan breaks open the cage of his mind,
all the birds fly in different directions.

### Akıl - Mind

An intelligent human being
cannot say all what he thinks,
but he will think about what he says.

### Kanaat - Conviction

Nobody has died because he was satisfied;
and nobody has become a king because of his passion.

### Hırs - Ambition

Passion makes human beings blind,
feeble, forces them to become ignorant,
and opens the way to a quick end, to death.

### Tövbe - Repentance

To ride the horse of repentance is a most miraculous thing;
it may jump from the shabbiest of the worlds
to the firmament.

### Sabır - Patience

Patience is the key to joy.

### Sabır - Patience

Patience is an iron shield.

### Sabır - Patience

Space comes from patience.

### Tecrübe - Experience

Those who live in hardship
and suffer arduous diseases,
appreciate the help of a doctor more deeply.

### Hırs - Ambition

Passion makes us live less
than a human being who keeps free of passion –
like a green tree which drinks water of the mortal life;
it soon turns yellow and fades away.

### Gerçekler - Reality

The Sun which travels through the entire universe
cannot hide its light because of the bats
who cannot bear the sunlight.

### Sevgi - Love

You look for the one you love;
you love the one who looks for you.

### Gönül - Heart

It is not allowed
to make your soul starve of its nourishment.

### Gönül - Heart

When the mirror of the soul is clean,
it can distinguish a beautiful face
from an ugly face.

### Dost - Friend

Do not listen to words
which separate you from your friend;
there is great loss in such words.

### Gayret - Strife

The efforts of a human being are his wings.

### Benlik - Egoism

When you eradicate your ego,
you will be master over all egos;
you can be a friend to every being,
even when they are not friendly to you.

### Kapasite - Capacity

You can really become rich!
But you can eat only
as much as you can digest.
You can plunge your jug completely in the ocean,
but it will only contain
as much water as the jug holds.

### Eylem - Action

Action comes from doing,
not from talking.

### Nasihat - Advice

The one who relies on his intuition
will not need advice from others.

### Performans - Performance

A dead man cannot appreciate the value of a doctor.

### Dost - Friend

When a human being is not able to recognise a friend
and distinguish a friend from a foe,
he would better be blind.

### Söz - Word

When your word does not bring a blessing,
better don't say it.

### Şekilcilik - Formalism

When you focus on form and appearance,
you cannot see; go beyond appearance,
look for the meaning of essence.

### Savaş - War

The wars human beings fight
are like children's quarrels,
all are meaningless and absurd.

### Iyilik - Goodness

When you begin to look for goodness,
all evil leaves you.

### Allah için - for God

Give your service to God,
do not look at whether others
will give theirs or not.

### Dinlemek - Listening

Speech should be attuned
to the one who is listening;
a tailor makes a suit
to match the size of the one who wears it.

### Adalet - Justice

When you don't understand about justice,
you are like the one who feeds a young wolf.

### Hile - Deceit

A wolf is really cruel,
but he does not deceive.

### Asalak - Parasite

You are like a worm in this apple;
you are neither aware of the tree
nor can you know the gardener.

### Güç - Strength

Water is victorious over fire;
but when you put water into a pot,
then the fire boils it and the water evaporates.

### Merhamet - Compassion

If you wish to reach compassion,
learn to be compassionate with the powerless.

### Kapitalist - Capitalist

Hey son, let go, free yourself from the tie!
Or do you want to become a slave of gold and silver?

### Nefis - Ego

Your ego likes the trap within yourself;
and this is worse
than all outer antagonism and arrogance.

### Ahmaklik - Stupidity

Nobody wonders when a sheep
runs away from the wolf;
all are surprised when the sheep loves a wolf.

### Asalet - Nobility

When vinegar becomes sourer,
the sweeter sugar must therefore become.

### Aşk - Love

Love is like a court case;
suffering has its attraction;
be conscious of it, if you wish to gain.

### Öz - Essence

What is inside the jug
will come out of it
in just the same condition.

### Kalp - Heart

Even with your capacity to reason,
your situation is difficult;
but when you don't listen to your heart,
you are hopeless.

### Peşin Hüküm - Prejudice

Do not despise any human being,
he might become a believer.
What do we know about the end of our lives?
So do not despise anyone.

### Ümit - Hope

Don't walk to the country of hopelessness
when there is hope,
don't walk into darkness
when there is the sun.

### Gerçek - Reality

Although a blind human being
cannot see the stars,
they are there all the same.

### Ölçü - Measure

Can a mirror or a scale tell a lie?

### Safiyet - Purity

When a river runs without ice or dirt,
it is truly beautiful.

### Kötüler - Bad People

Hey man, when you look for thorns
and come to heaven, just know
that you are the only one with thorns there.

### Yüzeysellik - Superficiality

When science is reflected in your heart,
you are supported by it,
but if it only pleases your brain,
it will become a load to you.

### Yaşam - Life

The greatest achievement for a human being
is to live his life fully.

### Duygu - Feeling

When human beings share their feelings,
they can agree and attune easily;
words of two people alone
do not meet the same language.

### Bakış açısı - Viewpoint

If all human beings would see the world
in the same way,
they could not see anything at all.

### İnsan - Human Being

You will learn to know a human being
by what he is interested in.

### Edep - Dignity

Dignity lightens up
the dark night of the world.

### Gönül - Heart

It is better to be a slave with an open heart
than to be dust on the head of a sultan.

### Gözyaşı - Tears

Tears show your compassion;
only when your heart is burning with love,
your eyes can cry.

### Veda - Farewell

When you are separated from your friend,
the wink of an eyelid feels like an entire year.

### Etki-Tepki - Impulse-Echo

This world is like a mountain;
it reflects an echo to all your actions.

### Söz - Word

Flattering words are like a sharp sword;
so hold a shield before you,
or stay far from them.

### Aşk - Love

Love is an infinite ocean,
there is no beginning and no end.

### Söz - Word

There are thousands of padlocks,
each of them wider than the horizon.
But two or three tender words,
like the teeth of a key,
can open such padlocks.

### Insan - Human Being

A human being cannot resound,
just like a reed,
as long he has not been hollowed.

### Öz - Essence

Can a young tree grow
from an infertile seed?

### Sevgi - Love

Love transforms pain into joy,
turns copper into gold;
dirty and shallow waters turn
sparkling, clean and fresh.

### Söz - Word

You will find a human being
hidden under his words.

### Öze Dönüş - Back to Essence

The Essence of all science
is the answer to the question:
'Who will I be on Judgment Day
and what will I become?'

### Kusur - Defect

When a human being becomes aware of his shortcomings,
he gallops towards maturity
and rides on ten horses for it.

### Şükür - Gratitude

Blessing as an answer to our gratitude
is more beautiful
than gratitude itself.

### Kadın - Woman

Some men marry women
and become as rich as Croesus.
Other men fall into debts
because of a woman.

### Akıl - Mind

A foolish friend
is at the same time
already your enemy.

### Allah'ın yardımı - Help of God

A human being who refuses God to help him,
believes to stand in front of a lion
where there is only a rabbit.

### Düşmanlık - Enmity

If the earth would become an enemy of the heavens
it would soon turn into a desert and die.

### Tedbir - Measure

Before taking a first step,
I watch where my foot will step onto.
So I keep myself from errors and from falling.

### Etme–Bulmadünyasi - You will find what you seek

If you wish to stay free from the influence of evil of others,
you must keep yourself from talking evil,
from teaching evil, and from thinking evil.

### Karakter - Character

A cat is king over the ones
who behave like rats.

### Öz - Essence

If you wish to see the colour of a cow,
look at her from outside;
but you will find
the colour of a human being inside.

### Sabır - Patience

Patience is the key to happiness,
hurry is the key to regret.

### Dil - Language

A human being can conquer the world,
but he cannot be master over his words.

### Gerçek - Reality

Don't sing a song in a dull bazaar,
and don't sell a mirror to a blind human being.

### Idrak - Understanding

It is foolish to say that all is right,
but we become dogmatic
when we say all is wrong.

### Ahmak - Fool

With a fool
silence is the best answer.

### Zenginler - Richness

Being rich gives you more commodities
than an ocean holds;
but you must be the ship on that ocean.

### Ahmak - Fool

If you are looking for something
you must go to the place where you can find it.

### Karakter - Character

Even though a stone may see a thousand springs,
it cannot turn green.

### Anne - Mother

A nurse is for three or four days;
but a mother raises us
and holds us close to her heart.

### Idrak - Understanding

The way you look,
is the way you see.

### Takım çalışması - Teamwork

Birds can only fly
with their own kith and kin.

### Peygamberler - Prophets

The prophets reveal God's commands to human beings,
and God Himself rewards them for their work.

### Eylem - Action

When you place an empty jug
close to a running spring,
it does not mean that it will be filled,
not even in forty years.

### Cehalet - Ignorance

A donkey pisses into a pit, then some straw falls on top of it;
a fly lands on this straw and has a feeling
as if she were sailing the ocean.
This is the best way to describe
idle knowledge and arrogant ignorance.

### Dost - Friend

Hey, this is your friend,
he is not something to be consumed,
please don't hurt him.

### Dünya - World

The world and the hereafter
are like two wives for a man.
He reconciles one,
and the other will reproach him for exactly that.

### Dost - Friend

The friend of the rose is the thorn.

### Insan - Human Being

Hey Brother,
thoughts and ideas are the essence of your being,
they make you human.
All other elements, bones and nerves,
animals also possess.

### Asalet - Nobility

Plain grass grows in two months' time,
but a red rose needs a full year to grow.

### Gözyaşı - Tears

When you are dirty within,
you cannot use water to cleanse,
it needs tears to purify.

### Doğruluk - Justice

Be straightforward as an arrow
and launch yourself from the bow.
Because no doubt, every arrow will leave the bow.

### Öze Dönüş - Return to Essence

Before we begin to read from books,
we should learn to read ourselves.

### Iyiler-Kötüler - Good Ones and Villains

A pitcher is afraid of a stone.

### Empati - Compassion

Oh man, you see the black spot
on the face of your neighbour!
What you see is a reflection of your own spot,
so don't hate it!

### Dost - Friend

Could you say that friendship is toil and hardship?
The heaviness lies inside, in the soul.
Friendship is like your skin, friendship stands firm
in difficulties and disasters.
A friend is like gold,
and also evil can be transformed into purity.

### Allah'ın yardımı - Help of God

In easy times all your companions are your good friends,
but at a certain moment
there will be no more companion except God.

### Güzel Söz - Fine Word

The songs of the nightingale are famous;
this is why she is kept in a cage.
But who would put crows or an owl into a cage?

### Gerçek - Facts

When you place two fingertips on your eyes,
can you see anything of the world?
The world does not exist, when you cannot see it.

### Gerçek - Facts

I wandered and searched the whole world,
but I could not find anything better than good manners.

### Alınteri - Effort

We closed the beggar's door for our companions.
Our friends earn their living in trade, science, craftsmanship,
any work honestly done, manual labour and sweat.
We follow Hz. Muhammed's suggestions:
'Expect from others what you are ready to give yourselves'.
If we disciples do not hold on to this ideal,
there is no joy on our path.

### Karakter - Character

Both reeds hold water,
yet one is completely empty,
and the other is full of sweetness.

### Karakter - Character

Donkeys will not reject sugar,
but they prefer grass, according to their nature.

### Takım çalışması - Teamwork

If you throw earth at someone's head, nothing happens.
If you pour water over someone's head, nothing happens.
If you want to crack the nut,
you must mix earth and water
and make a tile out of it.

### Fedakârlık - Selflessness

What is the value of gold,
of life, of a pearl, or a coral?
All are entirely worthless
if you are not ready to give out of love,
and to sacrifice them for a friend.

### Keder - Dreariness

You see, only dimwits remember me,
so a thousand times bravo to the dimwits.

### Fikir - Thought

A straight thought opens a path,
and it is called a path,
because it reaches reality.

### Sabır - Patience

Patience is the key
to freeing yourself from ignorance.

### Ayıplari Örtmek - Hide Your Faults

Hide your faults,
so your friends will cover your shame.

### Az konuşmak - Speak Little

A human being with deep thoughts speaks little.
The more superficial, the more essence gets lost.

### Öz - Essence

A purse or a leather bag
have not much value,
unless they are filled with gold.

### Bilgi - Knowledge

Check! What is inside the jug,
will also pour out of it.

### Kötüler - Villains

A twisted shoe
matches with a club-foot.

### Sabır - Patience

God has created a hundred thousand medicines,
chemical help for human beings;
but there is no medicine like patience.

### Cehalet - Ignorance

The purpose of a book lies in the information it contains,
but you can also use it as a pillow under your head.
It would be like beating with your hammer on the wall
instead of onto the nail.

### Eylem - Action

A living example in doing
is better than spoken advice.

### Gönül kırma - A Broken Heart

Never hurt the spirit of the needy.
God says: 'Don't hurt the needy,
never refuse a human being who asks for help.'
A wall says to the nail:
'Why do you disturb and hurt me?'
And the nail answers:
'Look at the one who slams his hammer on me'.

### Sorumluluk Bilinci - Conscious of Responsibility

When you know that you have done wrong,
you cannot cure it simply by saying sorry
or taking some medicine.

### Zulüm - Cruelty

When you dig a poisoned well of cruelty,
know that you are digging it for yourself.
Don't weave a cocoon around yourself like a silkworm.
If you wish to dig a well,
dig a well of peace which matches your size.

### Karakter - Character

A sharp sword
cannot cut soft silk.

### Gönül - Heart

As long as your heart does not burn,
your eyes cannot cry.

### Sabır - Patience

When you walk into a challenge wholeheartedly
and life turns narrow there, be patient!
Endurance is the key to wide space.

### Edep - Good Behaviour

The difference between a human being
and an animal is manners.

### Sevgi - Love

Look at this life in the world, Lord Almighty!
In whom of Your creatures have
Your loving arms grown mature?
So many prefer to go through life
kicking and slapping others,
they hardly embrace and give comfort.

### Insan - Human Being

Take care to know human beings well;
therefore, don't blame the one to be bad,
and don't glorify the other to be good.

### Kanaat - Conviction

I was worried
because I did not have any shoes;
but then I saw a man across the road,
and he had no legs.

### Gerçek - Reality

When you cannot see the hand,
you guess that the pen writes by itself.

### Dost - Friend

Once you have become one with the Friend,
both, life and death, become joyful.

### Merhamet - Compassion

Love and compassion are human traits,
anger and greed are animal traits.

### Gönül - Heart

Can your hands do something secretly,
and your spirit does not notice it?

### Kıymet - Value

When the hands of a child
hold the smell of onions,
how can it know what an apple is,
if it cannot see it?

### Güzellik - Beauty

When beauty is yours,
remember that it is borrowed.

### Güç - Power

When crows shout loudly,
the nightingales interrupt their song.

### Ömür - Life

We go through this life,
either busy with filling our pockets with money,
with greed for good eating and drinking,
or we are aware of the fact
that each and every breath of ours is counted.

### Karakter - Character

We told you –
a shepherd can become a wolf,
and a guard can become a thief.

### Kötü Huylar - Bad Character

Do not make bad habits your custom,
they take root in you and stay with you.

### Öğüt - Advice

An intelligent human being learns
from the warnings of evil
and considers death as his friend.

## Haddini Bilmek - Know Your Limits

The ocean does not become dirty,
because the lips of a dog touch the seawater.

## Şükür - Gratitude

Did you have to pay for the religion
you inherited from your father?
So why are you not grateful to God?
He gave it to you for free.
Is there a human being
who is really conscious of this privilege?

## Dost - Friend

Become a friend to human beings.
When the caravan is too crowded,
people tend to become very slow.

## Denge - Balance

A ship is built
to swim on the water,
but when water fills the ship, it will sink.
For a believer the world is the same as the water.

## Fikir - Thought

When your thoughts are like roses,
you will be like a rose-garden.
When your thoughts are thorny,
you are like the dry wood
which will be thrown into the fire.

### Adalet - Justice

What is justice?
To water the trees.
What is cruelty?
To water thorns.
Justice brings blessings to flow,
not water to irrigate all seeds.
What is cruelty?
To use improperly what is given to you,
to put a thing in an improper place.

### Ahlak - Morals

The human being who is ignorant is like iron;
when he uses his intelligence to learn about morals,
he will turn into gold.

### Asalet - Nobility

When a lion steals the prey of his neighbour,
he is ashamed,
but a dog will not feel shame.

### Zorba - Rowdy

When he says, everything is okay, he is a rowdy;
when he says everything is wrong, he is despotic.

### Aşk - Love

When love flows from the heart,
it accepts all suffering
and expects no return.

### Ayrılık - Separation

What is the wind for the fire?
Separation is the same for love;
it blows out a small love,
and it makes a great love stronger.

### Denge - Balance

If you never care to bring new water
when you keep taking away,
even the sea will dry out
and turn into a desert.

### Arzular - Desire

Pain arises from desire
which you cannot attain.

### Doğruluk - Justice

Truth does not need to run for justification.

### Dost - Friend

Go and see your friends regularly;
if you don't, on the road to them
may grow thorns and bushes.

### Dil - Tongue

The tongue is both,
unfathomable treasure
and incurable disease.

### Denge - Balance

A human being who speaks without thinking
is like a hunter who forgets to aim.

### Karakter - Character

Not every thorny bush
brings forth roses.

### Hayalperestlik - Don Quichotte Ride

If your pen was of wind
and your paper of water;
whatever you write will get lost.

### Dünya - Welt

We came naked,
we learned to dress;
then we undress
and now we leave.

### Sevgi - Love

The reason why a rose smells so beautifully
is that she is friendly to the thorn.

### Arzular - Desire

Winds often blow from directions
which the ship does not really like.

### Karakter - Character

If a donkey was a customer
and wished to buy something,
it would surely buy a melon.

### Kıymet - Value

Many gather around a well of fresh water.

### Bakış açısı - Viewpoint

The way you look
is the way you see.

### Tamah - Greed

If a mirror would become greedy,
it would twist
and could not show us
every detail as it really is.

### Arkadaş - Companion

If you wish to know your companion,
look who his friends are.

### Dikkat - Take Care

Even a dog
who eats a thrown away bone
and bread on top,
will stay with a smell of carrion.

### Karakter - Character

The human being whose nature and character is impure and ill, cannot accept anything good from anyone.

### Fikir özgürlüğü - Freedom of Thought

The thoughts of human beings
are like free birds in the sky,
you can neither catch
nor imprison them.

### Hata - Fault

If every sin
made a human being drunk,
you could not find anyone sober.

### Söz - Word

When you hold long speeches
it means that you cannot explain what you mean.

### Ömür - Life

The biggest loss in life
is to waste it with nonsense.
You cannot bring back one single year,
even if you pay a hundred thousand dinars.

### Iyilik - Goodness

Sow seeds of goodness, whenever you can;
without sowing no harvest will be possible.

### Kitap - Book

The book is nourishment for the soul
and medicine for the mind.

### Kötüler - Villains

If you pity thieves and villains,
it means to destroy human beings
who have no means to defend themselves.

### Muhammad

I would need a mouth,
wide as the sky,
so I would praise our Prophet
until the angels would become jealous.

### Aşk - Love

To give is an honour for the one who loves.
So sacrificing your life is generosity in love.

### Dünya - World

Not all human beings live in comfort,
have possessions and gold;
so why can you not share?
You do not even possess your own life,
so what hinders you to share?

### Dost - Friend

When a day passes
without seeing the face of our Friend,
it is like death or sleep.

### Dün-Bugün - Yesterday-Today

Oh my friend; yesterday is gone;
all we said, and all that is related to yesterday.
Today we must speak about
what is entirely new.

### Dikkat - Watch Out

When my eyes focus on the far horizon,
I cannot see the traps and pits before me:
What shall I do then?

### Gözyaşı - Tears

Wherever a river reaches,
the land turns green;
where tear-drops fall,
God's mercy and grace pours down.

### Dost - Friend

Dear friend, let us verify
what we mean for one another;
we might suddenly die and be separated

### Acele - Hurry

When you run you disturb your work;
what you wish to do, do it slowly and firmly.
Remember God gives maturity to human beings
over a period of forty years.

### Kötü Huylar - Bad Character

Hey, you know that bad manners
and a pretty face do not go together.

### Çalışmak - Work

To be successful in life,
you have three things at your disposal:
Attention, order and work.

### Gıpta - Envy

Do not envy others;
so there will be many
who will envy you
to live a good life.

### Allah'a Kulluk - To Serve God

Every human being is relieved
when he is free of slavery and forced labour.
But I find the greatest happiness
in serving God.

### Olgunlaşmak - Ripening

When young birds wish to fly
and their wings have not grown,
they become the prey of a greedy cat.

### Sabır - Patience

Patience is bitter,
but it brings sweet fruit.

### Taklit - Imitation

A parrot parrots.
But a human being always seeks
the Right, the Good and the Beautiful.
His careful selecting makes him human.

### Sır - Secret

If you entrust your secret
to a chatterbox,
it is like pouring water
into a cracked pot.

### Ömür - Life

When you look at life
as if it were a gold purse,
day and night will be robbers.

### Aşk - Love

When we have wandered through seven cities of love,
we still stand at the first step of the first road.

### Doğru - Right

It is difficult to say
what is right.

### Hırs - Greed

So many fish live in the water
and are safe;
only because of their greed for the bait
they get caught.

### Sevgi - Love

The worst people are both,
allergic and haggish.

### Iyilik - Goodness

When you are happy,
you give happiness to your fellow human beings;
when you are worried,
you bring worries to them.

### Söz - Word

The words of a human being disclose
what is in his heart.

### Kalp - Heart

Even when your coat is old,
your heart will always be
new, fresh and clean.

### Terbiye - Taming

Education is attitude of mind.

### Tevazu - Humility

I desired majesty,
and I found it in humility.

### Iyi Huy - Fineness

Become strong without violence,
and become soft
without becoming vulnerable.

### Cömertlik - Generosity

When you give freely,
you will become a generous human being.

### Vicdan - Conscience

The watchful observer of our bad deeds
is our own conscience.

### Ziyaret - Visit

Frequent visits make us tired,
few visits bring doubt to our friendship.

### Zulüm - Cruelty

Even when you are faced with a thousand cruelties,
never allow yourself to be cruel,
neither to yourself nor to others.

### Etki-Tepki - Action-Reaction

The World is like a mountain,
our actions produce a sound;
when we shout strongly at the mountain,
its echo will come back to us with the same impact.

### Kalp - Heart

The brotherhood of human beings in the heart
is higher than what they agree on in words.

### Komşu - Neighbours

Good neighbours are better than careless relatives.

### Dost - Friend

The blow of a friend hurts.

### Kitap - Book

One single library
makes an entire prison unnecessary.

### Kitap - Book

A home without books
is like a body without a soul.

### Kitap - Book

Those books help us
which push us to think deeply.

### Kitap - Book

Books are like plants
which never wither and fade.

### Kitap - Book

A book is like a letter
sent to the future.

### Dua - Prayer

When your heart is broken,
raise your hands in prayer.
Because God gives all his mercy
and compassion to the broken-hearted.

### Anne - Mother

When you are not thankful to your mother,
you are not thankful to God.
Without any doubt, her right is also God's right.

### Kader - Destiny

When you try to fight your fate,
to cut her head, you will fall,
and you will find yourself in your own blood.

### Öfke - Anger

Your anger is the seed of hell-fire.
Bring water, tame yourself and extinguish this hell!

### Gerçekler - Realities

The eye which looks at the ocean sees one thing,
the eye which looks at the foam sees something else;
give up the foam and look at the ocean.

### Dua - Prayer

The prayer of the pure-hearted
is free from disease and reaches God,
who is Greatness; and his prayer will be accepted.

### Nimet - Blessing

Be conscious and watchful
towards His Beneficence.
Who would give a blessing to someone
who is not even grateful?

### Allah'ın yardımı - Help of God

Even when you are a Sultan, King or Queen;
your greed keeps you away from God's Compassion.

### Kötü kişiler - Bad People

Evil becomes a habit to poor people.
Do them a favour, and they will give evil in return.

### Kaza - Accident

When an accident hits us,
it blinds our eyes
and we cannot even distinguish
between foot and head.

### Doğru söz - The Right Word

The right word brings relief to our heart.
Right words come out of good work from the heart.

### Dua - Prayer

When you pray carelessly,
you remain cold and worthless.
Careful prayers come
from a warm heart and love.

### Sevgi - Love

Love is a quality of human compassion;
anger and lust are characteristics of animals.

### Kanaat - Conviction

The Prophet says that conviction is a treasure.
Can everyone reach this hidden treasure?

### Tövbe - Repentance

When you feel
that your life is passing from you,
remember your roots.
Hurry and water your life tree
with water of repentance.

### Gönül - Heart

Oh you pure and virtuous beings!
A smile is hidden in a pure cry!
Go and search for this treasure in the old ruins!

### Takım çalışması - Teamwork

If one of our sayings is considered beautiful,
it is because of the one who listens.
A teacher puts all his soul and heart
into his work because of his student

### Heva Heves - Desire

Doubtlessly giving up desire is painful;
but pain is better
than being separated from God.

### Iyi Huy - Fine Character

Always stay close to human beings of fine character.
Look at the rose oil, how it has become one
with the character of the rose!

## Hz Muhammad

The holy Qur'an is like my skin,
as long as I am alive.

I am earth of the Prophet Mohammed's path;
he is the chosen One of God.
Whoever does not feel like this I pity
and cannot understand what he says.

Oh Mustafa!
Be the captain of this ocean of joy!
Because you are another Noah.
Intellects should be guided,
especially when we travel on the sea!

You are Khidr of our time,
you reach out to every ship in need.
You are like a lighthouse before this humanity,
you shine like the sun.

Oh, Prophet!
The right path is like the mountain Kaf, and you are phoenix.

Oh You Cure!
Let us not take advantage of patients,
let us not use the stick of a blind
to fall in anger and become deaf;
let us bring peace to the ones
who don't see in this world.

### Af - Forgiving

When you want to get out of trouble,
do not complain.
Hold on to your being generous,
forgiving, and goodhearted

### Sadaka - Alms

When you are giving,
your property never becomes less.
Being good never diminishes,
it saves you from losing yourself.

### Ölüm - Death

Birds drop dead in a cage,
so the owner takes them out,
and they fly free;
so will it be for me,
when I will depart from this world.

### Gönül - Heart

When roses grow in the earth,
they will flourish and wither.
Look how beautiful and everlasting
are the roses which grow in our heart!

### Güç - Power

There is a veil before the sun
because it is so intensely shining and active.

### Dost - Friend

Your possessions don't come with you,
they do not even follow you out of your house;
but your friend will come with you,
even to your grave.

### Eylem - Activity

Neither hazelnuts nor walnuts
show you what is inside them;
neither do they give out their oil
unless you break them.

### Hoşgörü - Tolerance

There are various forms of nearness.
The sun shines on mountains, on sand and on gold.
The sun feels close to both,
to a dry or a wet branch.

### Özlem - Longing

I am worried about the longing of my soul,
I would like to explain her,
step by step, what would help her
to overcome this feeling of separation.

### Dinlemek - Listening

When you speak, don't strive for superiority.
Listening stands higher than speaking.

### Sanat - Art

When we look at art
we will see that it was certainly a master
who taught the wisdom of art.

### Deli - Madness

When you take the weapon
from the hands of a madman,
you will be blessed with peace.

### Inanç - Belief

When belief enlightens your mind
you will guard righteousness;
so it will be the protector of the city of your heart,
and also its sovereign.

### Zaman - Time

Don't say, I will do it tomorrow;
so many 'tomorrows' are gone already.
Be awake that you don't miss the time of planting.

### Acele - Hurry

When you go slowly,
the light of God is with you;
when you hurry,
you react to the kick of a devil.

### Şehvet - Sensuality

A noble mind keeps its senses fine and alive.
Raw lust does not allow you to stand on your feet.

### Takım çalışması - Teamwork

How can the green grass smile
when the clouds don't cry?
How can milk gush forth from mother's breast
when the child does not cry?

### Sanat - Art

Hey wise one!
When you wish to reach true art,
help all others to attain it.

### Eğitim - Education

Many children to not like to go to school;
it is because they cannot yet grasp
the benefit of going to school.

### Allah - God

There is no better castle than to dwell in God;
make this castle your country.

### Sanat - Art

Hey brother, look for the mother-of-pearl
when you wish to see the art of a master.

### Teçrübe - Experience

The mind of an old human being has two wings;
even if he runs he flies with them to the sublime.

### Vatan Sevgisi - Love of your Country

Those who lack purity and decency
cannot feel love for their country;
so it is wise to stay far from them.

### Dünya - World

A human being in the world is poor and scared;
there is no reason to be afraid of thieves.
We come naked to this world and we go naked,
so why be afraid that someone takes from you?

### Verim - Result

Be sky, be cloud, and you will rain.
The drain pipe also becomes wet, but there is no benefit.

### Mesnevi - Mathnawî

When you are thirsty and you swim in the ocean,
the Mathnawi has opened a window,
from the ocean to your inner room.

### Dost - Friend

Many fall for the sweet words of an ignorant.
These words are like old rotten wine.

### Gayret - Effort

We have our destiny,
and we have our active work in the world;
let us listen within what is what.
We should not be as blind as a devil.

### Sabır - Patience

The quietness of the moon in the night
brings out its light.
The patience of the rose towards her thorns
brings forth her beautiful fragrance.

### Gönül - Heart

The one who is separated from his true friend
has no voice, even if he sings a hundred songs.

### Söz - Word

Once a word has gone beyond your lips,
it is like an arrow launched from the bow;
it will never return.

### Gönül - Heart

Your heart takes you
to the land of peace of heart;
your body holds you limited
between earth and water.

### Güçsüzler - Powerless

Don't think
that powerless people have no helper;
when they need help,
the soldiers of heaven come.

### Aşk - Love

When you cannot feel the pain of love,
you are like a bird without wings.
What a pity for you!

### Ahid - Agreement

When your agreement is based on injustice,
it is like rotten roots.
A tree with rotten roots
will never produce any fruit.

### Allah aşkı - Love of God

Decide for the Love of God,
because all prophets have been
blessed with glory and honour because of it.

### Bakış açısı - Viewpoint

A child is scared of the scalpel of a surgeon;
but the caring mother feels its pain
and helps it on to understand and feel relief.

### Sevgi - Liebe

Dust settles because of love,
pain is healed by love,
dead come to life through love,
a sultan turns into a slave because of love.

*   *   *

## Thank You

Well, dear friends, this was a wonderful year, these first nine months brought much water to be able to wash what threatens to get more and more stuck in our society. We are living amidst great changes, we cannot turn back the wheel of time; all the human beings who have come to us, they all live their lives here, in whichever category we put them.

We have drawn much water from the ocean, because we took it for granted that it would be ours anyway. Now we will need to fill it again, so that it will not degrade into a desert. We would need to deepen the riverbed.

I am so happy to have learned about 'Dost', and for all the human beings who taught me in this, my mouth is too small to show them my gratitude. So I just keep working on what has grown here, my form of showing gratitude; a year in my life, well used, with the joy to have brought more water than to have taken.

*'When we inquire deeply into life we find that what all souls seek is to know the meaning of life. The scientist looks and searches for it in the realm of science, and the artist finds it in his art. Whatever different interests people may have, their only real inclination is to find the meaning of life.'*

*'Destiny may be divided into two parts; one is the mechanism that activates the destiny, and the other part is the soul which realizes this. Therefore, the mechanism is the machine and the soul within is the engineer who is there to work this mechanism and to produce by it what is to be produced. There are many methods and ways which a human being adopts in order to know and understand; and the mind is the vehicle, the instrument, by the help of which he experiences life in the accomplishment of this purpose'*

These excerpts come from the teachings of a human being which brought me Mevlânâ Jelâleddin Rûm-î so close that I believe to have understood how we can work out beauty in our lives. Below I show the tools once more.

This is why this book has come to life, with exactly this wish:

### Kitap - Book

A book is like a letter,
sent to the future.

With most heartfelt greetings                    Puran

www.ingramcontent.com/pod-product-compliance
Lightning Source LLC
Chambersburg PA
CBHW070518090426
42735CB00012B/2827